This book is dedicated to a dear friend, mentor and like-minded person. E. Rick Nijs – King Rick (1961–2022).

He taught me three rules of thumb for a happy and adventurous life:

There's no place like home.
Think happy thoughts.
Maybe it's a day for a miracle.

FORTUNE COOKIE WISDOM

*Daily prophecies to manifest
your destiny*

DIRK JANSSENS

murdoch books
London | Sydney

CONTENTS

THE ORIGIN OF FORTUNE COOKIES

Fortune cookies have been associated with fortune and wisdom for centuries. The story goes that the first fortune cookies were made by Chinese monks in the fourteenth century. The monks used the cookies to share their message of wisdom and inspiration with people who came to see them in search of guidance and counsel.

Over time, fortune cookies increased in popularity, and traders ended up distributing them around the world. When Chinese immigrants arrived in the United States in the nineteenth century, they brought along the tradition of fortune cookies.

Fortune cookie sayings became mainstream when Chinese restaurants started serving the cookies. Prior to baking, small pieces of paper with predictive sayings and proverbs were hidden in the cookies. That's how every guest, opening a cookie, would end up with a unique message.

These days fortune cookies are still a popular treat in Chinese restaurants, and continue to form an important part of many Eastern and Western cultures.

HOW TO USE THIS BOOK

1. Hold the book in both hands.

2. Concentrate and open the book at a random page.

3. Read and discover your fortune cookie prediction or proverb.

4. Consult this book as often as you like.

5. Enjoy!

RECIPE FOR YOUR OWN FORTUNE COOKIES

INGREDIENTS:

2 egg whites
100 g (½ cup/3½ oz) granulated sugar
125 g (½ cup/4½ oz) butter, melted
60 ml (¼ cup/4½ fl oz) water
¼ teaspoon vanilla extract
¼ teaspoon almond extract
150 g (1 cup/5½ oz) plain flour
¼ teaspoon salt

REQUIRED:

Baking tray
Baking paper
Paper for your predictions or proverbs

INSTRUCTIONS:

1. Heat the oven to 180°C (350°F) and line a baking tray with baking paper.

2. Beat the egg whites and sugar until thick and fluffy.

3. Add the melted butter, water, vanilla extract and almond extract and mix well.

4. Add the flour and salt and mix all ingredients until you have a smooth batter.

5. Place a teaspoon of batter on the lined baking tray and form a circle with a 7 cm (2¾ in) diameter. Repeat with the remaining batter (you may need to work in batches or use more than one tray).

6. Bake for 6 to 8 minutes, or until the edges turn golden brown.

7. Quickly remove the cookies from the oven and place your paper with the prediction or proverb in the middle of each cookie.

8. Fold and press the edges of each cookie.

9. Bend and push each cookie into the shape of a crescent and let them cool.

10. Serve and enjoy your home-made fortune cookies.

200
AFFIRMATIONS

Believe in yourself and anything is possible

A day without laughter
is a day wasted

Fortune favours a
prepared mind

Work hard and act smart and success will come your way

A good deed is never wasted

By staying positive,
you will conquer
the storms of life

A plan without a
deadline remains
a dream

Real love can't be bought, only earned

Love is the key to
a happy life

A life without love
is like a garden
without flowers

A new chance at love
is on the horizon

Your new project will be
a success – go for it!

Your hard efforts will finally be rewarded

Soon a new love will
enter your life

You're about to experience an abundance of happiness

Happiness and joy
are at your door

A fantastic life
is within reach

Your future looks bright and full of new adventures

A good listener is someone who truly understands

A beautiful life is about to start

A long-held wish is
about to come true

If you want to see a rainbow, you must first withstand the rain

An amazing life
lies ahead

A large sum of money
is on its way to you

A big heart creates
a great life

Someone nearby has a
secret crush on you

A big dream will soon come true

A golden chance will come your way – seize it with both hands

A good reputation
is more valuable
than gold

An extraordinary,
beautiful life is just
around the corner

A sincere apology
can do wonders for a
broken relationship

A good deed will always be repaid – it may just take a while

Lady Luck is
on your side

Soon there will be
support from an
unexpected source

A grateful attitude is the key to happiness

A sincere apology
is the first step to
reconciliation

Lady Luck is about
to shine her beautiful
light on you

The most beautiful flowers often blossom unseen

Live life with passion and aspiration and everything will fall into place

Teaching someone
else is the best way
to learn yourself

A financial windfall
is coming your way

Sing if you want to scare
away your worries

Happiness is ready
to embrace you

This week, everyone will say 'yes' to your good ideas

Fortune will follow you
wherever you go

Anger is like a
stone thrown into
a hornet's nest

This week, love has lined up a date for you

Soon there will be
new chances and luck
in love

Tip your hat to the past and roll up your sleeves for the future

Open your heart to that
special person

Your future looks bright

Happiness will soon be
knocking on your door

If you're too afraid to roll the dice, you'll never score a six

Doubt no longer –
success is guaranteed!

These are your
lucky numbers:
3, 7, 9, 24, 29, 33

Unexpected love turns
your life upside down

Not all grey clouds mean rain

Money and happiness
will soon be yours
in abundance

The person who
always looks back
will never
move forward

Soon love will show its most beautiful side

A vague question
will always result in
a vague answer

An exciting encounter
will turn your life
upside down

Give and forget,
receive and remember

Someone will give you a chance to make your dream come true

Someone in your vicinity has a secret soft spot for you

Imagination is often more important than knowledge

Trust your intuition – it will show you the way

One can never really be happy at the expense of others

A long-cherished wish
is about to be fulfilled

Those who expect happiness will find it

A rich person is
one who knows
they have enough

A master of patience is a master of many things

A small fire warms;
a large fire destroys

An ending is never the end, but the beginning of something new

It's never too late to take a new path

With a positive attitude, happiness will appear on your path

Success will come when
you least expect it

Speech is silver,
silence is golden

Your dreams will come
true – be patient

A joyful attitude will
always protect you

Promising too much damages trust

The coming days will bring you delightful romance

You are made
of sunshine

You're better off ignoring an insult than avenging it

Let your heart be your compass and you will never get lost

A touch of luck
is literally around
the corner

Shortly you'll receive a nice financial reward

Time brings counsel;
love heals wounds

Don't put off until tomorrow what you can do today

Not answering can also
be an answer

Without an open mind, nothing new can enter your life

Happiness will
arrive quickly

Inner happiness
fuels success

Adversity brings experience, and experience brings insight

One of your hobbies is about to achieve great success

Good news is on
its way to you

Knowledge is the ultimate weapon against fear

Happiness and success await you soon

All your wishes are
about to be fulfilled

Happiness arrives when
you least expect it

You deserve a happy
and beautful life

Your day will be filled
with happiness and
abundance

A radiant smile is the key to a happy heart

Believe in yourself
and everything will go
according to plan

Dream big, work hard
and happiness will
follow

Happiness and love will knock on your door when you least expect it

Abundant moments
of happiness are
awaiting you

The sun will always
shine for you

Soon you'll achieve
wonderful success

Pleasant company, love
and blissful times are
on their way to you

Development of the soul
is as essential as food is
for the body

Wealth and success are written in the stars for you

Today will
bring wonders

Good news is about
to arrive

Kindness towards others will yield kindness in return

Sunny and happy days
are coming your way

The most simple solution is often the correct one

Walk with your head in the clouds, but keep your feet on the ground

You have an
attractive smile

All your problems
will disappear and
happiness will smile
upon you

You're never too old to choose a different path

Wisdom starts
with humility

Wherever you go, happiness will follow you

All your dreams will
come true

A brilliant future awaits you

Perhaps today is a day
for a miracle

Be joyous and happy –
you never know who
could fall in love with
your smile

Good times lie ahead

Make your move –
success is guaranteed!

Your life will be
filled with moments
of great joy

A time of happiness has arrived for you

A happy life awaits you

A friend is someone who knows everything about you and loves you unconditionally

Don't forget to love yourself

Believe in yourself and you will succeed

A positive attitude
opens the door
to happiness and
good luck

Giving more than you take will provide you with abundance

Treat others how you want to be treated

Don't look back –
focus on the now
and the future

You'll reap what
you sow

A beautiful future starts with a positive mindset

Profound happiness
is awaiting you

Your days will be filled
with love and joy

Be patient; happiness
still lies ahead

Passion and persistence
are keys to success

Your future looks extremely rosy

Never fret about your
financial matters

Cease doing things that don't make you happy

Listen to your heart –
that's where your real
feelings are

Big things can
start small

It's better to act out of love than out of fear

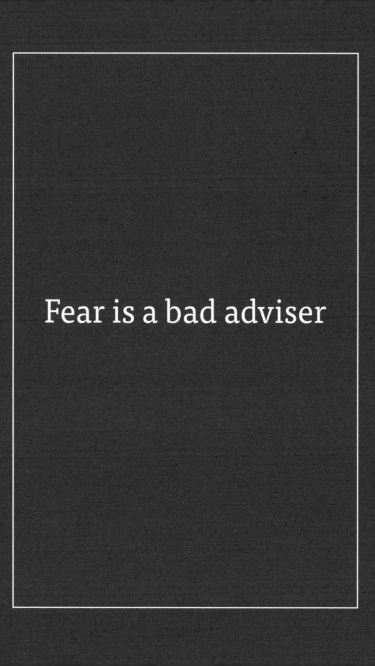

Fear is a bad adviser

Their heart belonged
to you the moment
you met

A good deed benefits your karma

Many of your dreams
will come true this year

All your wishes will
soon be fulfilled

Luck in love is quickly approaching

Love is the only thing
that grows when shared

Happiness is on
its way to you

Do something today
to make your future
self grateful

Small victories lead to big achievements

Your life is like a fortune cookie: full of pleasant surprises

Do something today
that will make you
grateful tomorrow

Trust that everything
will fall into place
at the right time

Those who are too careful are careless

A small effort can lead
to major results

The path of love will guide you to a beautful marriage

Life is looking out
for you

Good times are ahead

The key to a happy relationship is in your hands

Open your eyes to magic
and see a world full
of miracles

A bright future smiles
upon you

Like the body, the soul
requires nutrition

The love you spread
is the love you receive
in return

A bright future awaits you, full of unlimited possibilities and adventures

Soon your deepest wish
will be fulfilled

Live each day as if you are in love, then in love you will be

Soon all your wishes
will come true

Your choice will be
supported by many

Your life is about to take
a positive turn

Your patience will be richly rewarded

Nothing ventured,
nothing gained

Happiness occurs
when preparation and
opportunity converge

Don't worry – all will be well

Fun times are ahead

Today is the day to start something new

Big adventures start
with small steps

Your words can
be doubted; your
actions can't

A fantastic life is up for grabs

Beauty comes from within

Trust your intuition and it will guide you to a beautiful life

The secret of life is to appreciate what you have and to pursue what you desire

A wise person speaks less and listens more

Happiness isn't derived from possessions, but from experience and healthy relationships

Follow your heart –
that's where your
deepest desires lie

The thousand-mile journey starts with the first step

At an unexpected
moment, intense joy
will fall in your lap

Care for others and the world will care for you

A door to happiness will
open for you

Create a happy life

ACKNOWLEDGEMENTS

During our journey in life we all come across extraordinary people **who suddenly fill our hearts with a deep sense of joy.** *One could call them 'soul mates'. Some of those people appear for a reason, sometimes for a moment, sometimes for a complete lifetime.*

My sincere thanks to all the sources that contributed to the creation of this book, and particularly to Isabelle Moussiaux, Betty Haesendonck, Muriel Van den Bergh, E. Rick Nijs, Jan Merckx, Pieter Vandenhout, Maxime Van Melkebeke, Frank Smedts, Joris Persy, Thomas Richard Mertens, Koen Anteunis, Wim Dewulf, Elke Giets, Tineke Dierick, Claire Vanneste, David Zelikovsky, John Dabu and Abigail Flores for their friendship, humour, loyalty and unconditional support. I'm also grateful to my clients who believed in my art from day one.

You enlightened my path and warmed my heart.

Leuven, August 2023

Dirk Janssens

Published in 2024 by Murdoch Books, an imprint of Allen & Unwin.
First published as *Het Fortune Cookie Boek: 200 voorspellingen voor een dagelijkse dosis geluk en wijsheid* in 2023 by Lannoo Publishers (translated from the Dutch language).

Murdoch Books UK
Ormond House
26–27 Boswell Street
London WC1N 3JZ
Phone: +44 (0) 20 8785 5995
murdochbooks.co.uk
info@murdochbooks.co.uk

Murdoch Books Australia
Cammeraygal Country
83 Alexander Street
Crows Nest NSW 2065
Phone: +61 (0)2 8425 0100
murdochbooks.com.au
info@murdochbooks.com.au

For corporate orders and custom publishing, contact our business development team
at salesenquiries@murdochbooks.com.au

Text and proverbs: Dirk Janssens
Design: Studio Lannoo (Aurelie Matthys)

English-language publisher: Céline Hughes
English-language editorial manager: Breanna Blundell
English-language design manager: Megan Pigott
Translator: Eiko Bron
Production director: Lou Playfair

Text and design © Lannoo Publishers Ltd., Tielt, 2023
The moral right of the author has been asserted.
www.lannoo.com

Murdoch Books Australia acknowledges the Traditional Owners of the Country on which we live and work. We pay our respects to all Aboriginal and Torres Strait Islander Elders, past and present.

ISBN 978 1 76150 057 2

A catalogue record for this book is available from the British Library

 A catalogue record for this book is available from the National Library of Australia

Colour reproduction by Splitting Image Colour Studio Pty Ltd, Wantirna, Victoria
Printed by 1010 Printing International Limited, China

OVEN GUIDE: You may find cooking times vary depending on the oven you are using. The recipe in this book is based on a fan-assisted oven temperature. For non-fan-assisted ovens, as a general rule, set the oven temperature to 20°C (35°F) higher than indicated in the recipe.

DISCLAIMER: The content presented in this book is meant for inspiration and informational purposes only. The author and publisher claim no responsibility to any person or entity for any liability, loss, or damage caused or alleged to be caused directly or indirectly as a result of the use, application, or interpretation of the material in this book.

10 9 8 7 6 5 4 3 2 1

MIX
Paper | Supporting responsible forestry
FSC® C016973